J   745.5 ADD $5.95

Addy's craft book

1864

ADDY'S
CRAFT
BOOK

*A Look at
Crafts from the
Past with Projects
You Can Make Today*

PLEASANT COMPANY PUBLICATIONS, INC.

Published by Pleasant Company Publications Incorporated
© Copyright 1994 by Pleasant Company Incorporated

First Edition.
Printed in the United States of America.
94 95 96 97 98 99 WCR 10 9 8 7 6 5 4 3 2 1

PICTURE CREDITS
The following individuals and organizations have generously
given permission to reprint illustrations in this book:
Page 1—Collection of Eleanor Lee, Woodstock, New York; 4—Massachusetts
Commandery Military Order of the Loyal Legion and the U.S. Army Military History
Institute; 5—Library of Congress; 7—Reproduced by permission of the American
Museum in Britain, Bath ©; 10—Taken from *To Have and To Hold, Decorative American
Boxes,* by Pat Ross; 11—African American Images (left); Taken from *Paper Dolls* by
Anne Tolstoi Wallach (right); 13—Society for the Preservation of New England
Antiquities; 17—Courtesy of the Burton Historical Collection of the Detroit
Public Library; 18—Stagville Center, Division of Archives and History, North
Carolina Department of Cultural Resources; 19—American Museum in Britain (left);
Strong Museum (right); 21—Percy Muir Collection, *Derrick Witty;* 23—Moorland-
Spingarn Research Center, Howard University, Photographer: Allen and Rowell;
26—Louisiana State Museum; 27—Bequest of Maxim Karolik, Courtesy, Museum
of Fine Arts, Boston (left); National Portrait Gallery, Smithsonian Institution (right);
34—Photographs and Prints Division, Schomburg Center for Research in Black
Culture, The New York Public Library, Astor, Lenox and Tilden Foundations;
35—Strong Museum (left); Collection of Marna Anderson (right); 37—Photograph
courtesy of Blair Whitton, the author of the book *Paper Toys of the World;* 39—Anton
Gullick/Collection; 40—Taken from *String Figures and How to Make Them, A Study of
Cat's Cradle in Many Lands,* by Caroline Furness Jayne, Dover Publications, Inc., © 1962.

Edited by Jodi Evert
Written by Rebecca Sample Bernstein, Tamara England, and Jodi Evert
Designed and Art Directed by Jane S. Varda
Produced by Karen Bennett, Laura Paulini, and Pat Tuchscherer
Cover Illustration by Susan Mahal
Inside Illustrations by Geri Strigenz Bourget
Photography by Mark Salisbury
Historical and Picture Research by Polly Athan,
Rebecca Sample Bernstein, Jodi Evert, and Doreen Smith
Crafts Made by Jean doPico and June Pratt
Craft Testing Coordinated by Jean doPico
Prop Research by Leslie Cakora

Library of Congress Cataloging-in-Publication Data

Bernstein, Rebecca Sample.
Addy's craft book : a look at crafts from the past with projects you can make today /
[edited by Jodi Evert ; written by Rebecca Sample Bernstein, Tamara England, and Jodi
Evert ; inside illustration by Geri Strigenz Bourget ; photography by Mark Salisbury].
— 1st ed.
p. cm.
ISBN 1-56247-124-4 (softcover)
1. Handicraft—Juvenile literature. 2. United States—Social life and customs—19th
century—Juvenile literature. 3. Afro-Americans—History—19th century—Juvenile
literature. [1. Handicraft. 2. United States—Social life and customs—19th century.
3. Afro-Americans—History—19th century.] I. England, Tamara. II. Evert, Jodi.
III. Bourget, Geri Strigenz, ill. IV. Salisbury, Mark, ill. V. Title.
TT171.B47 1994 745.5—dc20 94-26045 CIP AC

CONTENTS

Special thanks to all the children and adults who tested the crafts and gave us their valuable comments:

Nicole Anderson and her mother Nancy Anderson
Alisa Brown and her mother Marlene Brown
Whitney Fahey and her mother Gail Fahey
Angela Dawn Fraser and her mother Janet Wells
Kirsten Fritz and her mother Debbie Fritz
Janessa Graves and her mother Debra Graves
Jana Hicks and her mother Shelly Hicks
Emily Holcomb and her mother Melissa Holcomb
Cassie Lee and her mother Debra Lee
Melissa Lindsay and her mother Patty Lindsay
Danielle Miles and her mother Dawn Miles
Samantha Jo Oscar and her mother Sue Oscar
Jillian Parish and her mother Sally Parish
Lindsay Polasek and her mother Lori Polasek
Christine Quale and her mother Monica Quale
Lauren Roberts and her mother Karen Roberts
Monica Saidler and her mother Elyse Saidler
Maria Schmitz and her mother Jean Tretow-Schmitz
Dawn Schwartz and her mother Shelley Schwartz
Jessa Sharkey and her mother Paulette Sharkey
Kelly Sloan and her mother Nancy Sloan
Amanda and Patti Steinhauer and their mother Mary Steinhauer
Rachel Tham and her mother Nancy Tham
Kelly Toltzien and her mother Paula Toltzien
Lindsay Trachtenberg and her mother Ann Trachtenberg
Jennifer Tuggle and her mother Terri Tuggle
Rachel Vitense and her mother Mary Vitense
Lindsay Wadleigh and her mother Barbara Wadleigh
Kari Lynn Walter and her mother Linda Walter

CRAFTS FROM THE PAST

In 1864, many African Americans were living in slavery on plantations in the South. Slaves were not paid for their work, and they could be sold away from their families at any time. They lived in small cabins or huts that they or their ancestors had built by hand.

Enslaved men and women were often skilled craftspeople. Women made baskets and soap by hand. Many women sewed clothes, quilts, blankets, and sheets using fabric they had woven and thread they had spun themselves. They also made some of their own fabric dyes from tree bark, nuts, and berries. Sometimes their sewn goods had traditional African shapes and patterns.

Men were often skilled carvers, potters, and blacksmiths. In fact, most skilled craftsmen in the South were African-American slaves. In the 1860s, the town of Tuskegee, Alabama, had 65 skilled craftsmen, including carpenters, blacksmiths, and shoemakers. They were all black men.

Some slaves escaped and brought their skills to the North, where they lived in free black communities. Former slaves sometimes were able to find work similar to the work they had done in the South. In the North, they were paid for their skills, often for the first time in their lives.

Learning how and why crafts were made long ago will help you understand life in Addy's time. Making the crafts she might have made will bring history alive for you today.

ADDY ☀ 1864

When Addy's family arrived in Philadelphia, they brought skills they had learned in the South, such as sewing and carpentry. Many African Americans also kept alive African traditions that had been passed down for generations, such as music, pottery, basketry, cooking, and dance.

A quilt made by slaves in the 1850s.

CRAFT TIPS

This list of tips gives you some hints about creating the crafts in this book. But this is the most important tip: **work with an adult**. The best thing about these crafts is the fun you will have making them together.

1. Choose a time that suits you and the adult who's working with you, so that you will both enjoy making crafts together.

2. You can find most of the materials listed in this book in your home or at craft and fabric stores. If an item in the materials list is starred (*), look at the bottom of the list to find out where you can get it.

3. If you don't have something you need or can't find it at the store, think of something similar you could use. You might just think of something that works even better!

4. Read the instructions for a craft all the way through before you start it. Look at the pictures. They will help you understand the steps.

5. If there's a step that doesn't make sense to you, try it out with a piece of scrap paper or fabric first. Sometimes acting it out helps.

6. Select a good work area for your craft project. Pick a place that has plenty of light and is out of reach of pets and younger brothers and sisters.

PAINTS AND BRUSHES

*You'll use water-based, or **acrylic**, paints to make some of the crafts in this book. Here are a few hints for using paints and brushes:*

☀ *Don't dip your brush into the paint bottle. Squeeze a little paint onto newspaper or a paper plate.*

☀ *Have a bowl of water handy to clean the brush each time you change colors.*

☀ *Make sure one color is dry before adding another.*

☀ *Clean your brush with soap and water and let it dry before you put it away.*

7. Wear an apron, tie back your hair, and roll up your sleeves. Cover your work area with newspapers and gather all the materials you will need before you start.

8. It pays to be careful. Be sure to get an adult's help when the instructions tell you to. Have an adult help you use tools properly. Don't use the stove or oven without an adult's permission.

9. Pay attention when using sharp knives and scissors so you don't cut your fingers! Remember—good, sharp knives and scissors are safer and easier to use than dull ones.

10. To prevent spills, put the covers back on containers tightly. If you do spill, clean it up right away.

11. If your craft doesn't turn out exactly like the picture in the book, that's terrific! The pictures are there just to give you ideas. Crafts become more meaningful when you add your own personal touch.

12. Cleanup is part of making crafts, too. Leave your work area as clean as you found it. Wash and dry dishes, trays, and tabletops. Sweep the floor. Throw away the garbage.

THREADING A NEEDLE

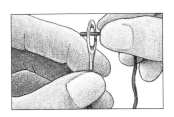

1. Wet the tip of the thread in your mouth. Then push the tip of the thread through the eye of the needle.

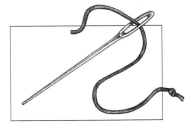

2. Pull about 5 inches of the thread through the needle. Then tie a double knot near the end of the long tail of thread.

HOME COMFORTS

A Georgia family outside their cabin in 1862.

On Master Stevens's plantation, Addy and her family lived in a cabin similar to the kind of house that pioneers built in the West. The Walkers' cabin had only one tiny room, and that's where Addy's family cooked, ate, and slept. The floor was made of packed dirt, and they had to sleep on itchy cornhusk mattresses on the floor. Still, Momma and Poppa managed to make their home a little more comfortable. Momma stitched the family's clothes and bed coverings, and Poppa built a sturdy table and chairs from wood scraps.

After Addy and Momma escaped to freedom in Philadelphia, Momma was hired as a seamstress. The money she earned for her skills helped them survive in the North. Momma's job brought them to a new home, too—the garret above Mrs. Ford's dress shop. The garret was tiny and dirty, but it had comforts that their cabin had lacked—a cast-iron cookstove, wood floors, and a real bed to sleep in. After Addy and Momma scrubbed it clean, the garret started to feel a little more like a home.

HOME COMFORTS

☀

Hooked Rug

•

Spatterwork Picture

After Poppa found Addy and Momma in Philadelphia, the Walkers moved into Mr. and Mrs. Golden's boarding house. Even though Addy and her family still lived in only one room, the boarding house also had a parlor that all the boarders shared. Addy's favorite thing in Mrs. Golden's parlor was the colorful hooked rug in front of the sofa. She was thrilled when Mrs. Golden gave her a scrap of canvas and taught her how to use a rug hook. The scrap was the perfect size to make a rug for her doll Ida Bean. Addy often worked on her doll rug in M'dear's room. While she listened to M'dear's stories, Addy hooked bits of yarn into a picture of Sunny, M'dear's pet canary!

ROW HOUSES

*In 1864, many families moved to the cities to find work. To save space in large cities like Philadelphia, houses were built with shared, or **party**, walls. These tall, narrow buildings, called **row houses**, were built so close together that they looked like books on a shelf.*

HOOKED RUG

Make a pretty hooked rug for your favorite doll.

MATERIALS

Black felt-tip marker
Tracing paper
Masking tape
Piece of rug canvas, 10 by 12 inches
Ruler
Latch hook
Rug yarn *(purple, tan, and yellow)*
Scissors
Straight pins
Heavy thread
Needle

DIRECTIONS

1. Trace the canary pattern shown on page 42 onto tracing paper. Don't cut it out. Tape the pattern to a table, design side up.

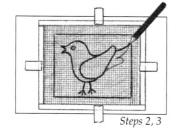

Steps 2, 3

2. Tape the edges of your rug canvas so they won't unravel. Place the rug canvas on top of the canary pattern. Center the canvas over the pattern, and then tape the canvas to the table.

3. Trace the pattern onto the rug canvas. Then draw a line 1 inch in from each edge. These lines mark the edges of your rug design.

4. Untape the canvas and the tracing paper pattern. Now you're ready to hook your rug.

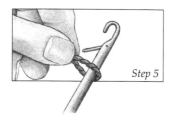

Step 5

5. To work the latch hook, hold it in 1 hand. Then fold a piece of purple yarn in half around the hook, just below the latch.

6. Begin in the square at the bottom right corner of the rug design. Push the hook under 1 of the horizontal canvas threads. Make sure the latch is open.

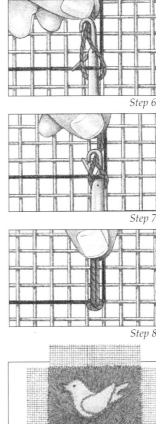
Step 6

7. Pull the yarn up as shown, and then pull the hook back toward you. The latch will close over the yarn.

Step 7

8. Pull the hook all the way back through the canvas. Then pull the yarn ends to make a knot.

Step 8

9. Hook the rest of the rug in the same way, working right to left. Work row by row from the bottom up, using purple yarn for the background, tan for the lines of the canary, and yellow inside the canary lines.

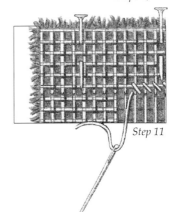
Steps 9, 10

10. When your design is complete, untape the edges of the canvas and cut out the corners as shown.

11. Turn over the rug. Pin the edges to the back of the rug, and then have an adult help you sew them down. Your rug is finished! ☀

Step 11

HANDMADE RUGS

In Addy's time, few families could afford to buy fine woven carpets. Working-class women hooked their own rugs from yarn or rags for warmth and decoration. Burlap was often used for the backs of rugs because it was inexpensive and sturdy.

SPATTERWORK PICTURE

It's easy to make a pretty picture for your room. Just spread out lots of newspaper and spatter away!

MATERIALS

Paint smock or old shirt
Newspapers
Pencil
3 sheets of white paper, each 8 by 10 inches
Scissors
Old toothbrush
Acrylic paints, any colors
Craft sticks
Small stones

DIRECTIONS

1. Spatterwork painting is messy! Wear a paint smock or old shirt and cover your entire work area with newspapers.

2. Use the pencil to draw a simple shape on paper to use as your spatter-paint pattern. Your pattern can be almost anything—a heart, a star, or your favorite animal. You can even use an animal pattern from the back of this book.

3. When you are happy with your pattern, cut it out and set it aside.

4. Place a sheet of practice paper on top of the newspapers. Dip the toothbrush bristles into 1 color of acrylic paint. Gently shake off the excess paint. You may have to thin the paint with a little water to make the paint a good consistency for spattering.

SPATTER-PAINTING

In the 1860s, women spatter-painted over pressed leaves and cut-out pictures. It was a simple way to give their furniture, throw pillows, and even lampshades, like the one shown above, a fresh look.

5. Try spattering your paint onto the practice paper. Hold a craft stick in 1 hand and the toothbrush in the other. Point the toothbrush toward the practice paper.

6. Beginning at the far end of the brush, slowly pull the craft stick across the bristles. A fine spray of paint will spatter onto your paper.

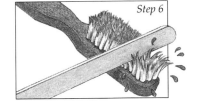

Step 6

7. When you've finished practicing, set your practice paper aside.

8. Place another sheet of paper on a clean part of your newspaper work area. Then place the cutout pattern on the center of the paper.

9. To hold down the pattern, place 1 stone in the center of the pattern and the others around the edges.

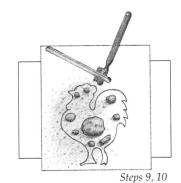

Steps 9, 10

10. Spatter-paint around the edge of the pattern, just as you practiced.

11. After the paint is dry, remove the paper cutout, and your spatterwork picture is finished!

12. Experiment with more than 1 paint color for each picture. Use a fresh craft stick and clean the toothbrush with water each time you change colors. Try spatter-painting over other designs, too! ☀

PAPER PASTIMES

Wallpaper boxes from Addy's time.

In Addy's time, girls made small wallpaper boxes by gluing wallpaper scraps onto plain wooden and cardboard boxes. Some people used large wallpaper boxes, called *bandboxes*, as luggage. In the mid-1800s, many bandboxes were made in factories, but others were handcrafted. A woman named Hannah Davis made beautiful bandboxes and sold them in many northern states. She *bartered*, or traded, with friends to get different wallpapers, and she lined each box with newspaper.

In Addy's time, improved printing machines

and papermaking techniques made books, magazines, and newspapers easier to produce. Children's novels and books of jokes and riddles became especially popular. Because books were easier to make than they had been, they became less expensive.

By 1870, almost 6,000 different magazines and newspapers were published in America. There was a magazine for almost any topic, from farming to fashion. And most towns had at least one newspaper. Some newspaper offices were very large, with many editors, writers, and printers. Smaller papers were often run by one person who wrote the stories, printed the paper, and delivered it to customers.

Anti-slavery newspapers were published from offices like this one in Addy's time.

In many northern cities, African-American communities produced their own newspapers. These newspapers were among the many ways black people helped one another. There were advertisements inviting readers to anti-slavery meetings and conventions, and there were articles on everything from successful business practices to household hints.

PAPER PASTIMES

☀

Wallpaper Box

•

Revolving Serpent

•

Animal Chains

PAPER DOLLS

*The first black paper dolls in the United States were produced in 1863. The dolls were characters from the anti-slavery book **Uncle Tom's Cabin**, written by Harriet Beecher Stowe. They were also the first paper dolls made to look like characters from a popular novel!*

WALLPAPER BOX

*This box is great for gift-giving.
You don't even need to wrap it!*

MATERIALS

Wallpaper*
Scissors
Round wooden or cardboard box, 4 to 5 inches wide,
   with lid
Pencil
White glue
Foam paintbrush, 1 inch wide
Tape measure

*Available in home decorating stores or in the home decorating
 section of some department stores.*

DIRECTIONS

1. Plan your design. If your wallpaper has an all-over pattern, you can cut it in any direction. But if it has stripes, you may want to plan the design so all the stripes go in the same direction.

2. Cut a piece of wallpaper a little bigger than your box lid. Then lay the paper on a table, design side down.

3. Place the lid upside down on the wallpaper. Trace around the lid and then cut out the shape.

4. Squeeze glue on the top of the lid. Use the paintbrush to spread it evenly until the whole top of the lid is covered with a thin coat of glue.

5. Glue the wallpaper, design side up, onto the lid. Rub gently across the top to smooth out bubbles.

6. To cover the sides of the lid, first measure the distance around the lid, or the *perimeter*. Write down that distance. Then measure how tall the side of the lid is, and write that down.

7. Ask an adult to help you cut a strip of wallpaper 1 inch longer than the perimeter of the lid and as wide as the height of the lid. If your lid has a 14-inch perimeter and is $\frac{1}{2}$ inch tall, cut a 15- by $\frac{1}{2}$-inch strip.

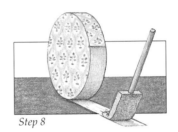

8. Lay the strip, design side down, on the table. Squeeze a thin line of glue along the strip. Use the foam paintbrush to spread the glue evenly over the strip. Wrap the strip around the side of the lid, smoothing out bubbles as you wrap.

Step 8

9. Have an adult help you cover the sides of the box the same way you covered the sides of the lid. Your box is finished! ☀

WALLPAPER

Wallpaper was very popular in Addy's time, and it came in many different designs. Some wallpapers looked like wood or stone. Others were decorated with flowers and landscapes or showed historic sites and important events. Some magazines even told people what wallpaper patterns were best for each room of a house!

REVOLVING SERPENT

Hold this spiraling serpent over a light bulb and watch it spin!

MATERIALS

Pencil
Tracing paper
Newspaper
Piece of construction paper, 5 by 8 inches
Transparent tape
Scissors
Thread, any color
Ruler
Needle
Crayons or markers *(optional)*
Paper scraps
White glue

DIRECTIONS

1. Use the pencil to trace the serpent pattern shown on the inside back cover of this book onto tracing paper. Don't cut out the pattern.

2. Place the tracing paper on the newspaper, design side down.

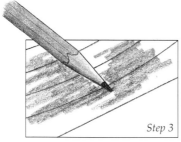

Step 3

3. Use the side of the pencil to color over the back of the serpent pattern. Color over the pattern completely.

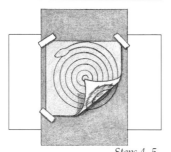

Steps 4, 5

4. Place the tracing paper on top of the construction paper, design side up. Tape it to the construction paper at the corners. Draw over the lines of the serpent pattern, pressing firmly.

5. Lift up the tracing paper. The pencil markings from the back of the tracing paper will come off where you traced.

6. Cut out the serpent. When you've finished, you'll have a spiral.

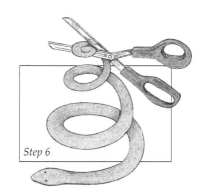

Step 6

7. Cut a 1-foot piece of thread, and thread the needle. Tie a double knot 2 inches from the other end of the thread.

8. Use the needle to make a hole through the serpent's tail, and then pull the thread through until the knot stops it.

Step 8

9. Trim off the extra thread below the knot. Make another double knot 2 inches from the needle and trim off the extra thread.

10. Color your serpent if you like. Use the paper scraps to make eyes and a slithery tongue. Glue them on, and then hold or tie your serpent a few inches above an electric light bulb.

11. Turn on the light. The heat from the bulb will make the serpent slowly spin around. ☀

LIGHTING

In the 1860s, there were no electric lights. Many people depended on candles and kerosene lamps for light. **Kerosene** *is a fuel made from* **petroleum**, *an oily liquid. The smoke from candles and kerosene lamps often left black marks on people's ceilings. So they used gadgets like the revolving serpent to fan the smoke away.*

ANIMAL CHAINS

*Make your own colorful parade
of circus animals!*

MATERIALS

Pencil
Tracing paper
Newspaper
Piece of construction paper, 2½ by 10 inches
Scissors

DIRECTIONS

1. Use the pencil to trace 1 of the small animal patterns on page 44 onto tracing paper. Don't cut out the pattern.

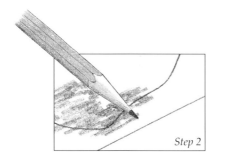
Step 2

2. Place the sheet of tracing paper onto newspaper, design side down. Use the side of the pencil to color over the lines of the pattern on the back of the tracing paper.

3. Place the tracing paper on the construction paper, design side up. Line up the animal's head with the edge of the paper.

4. Draw over the lines of the pattern, pressing firmly.

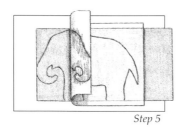
Step 5

5. Lift up the tracing paper. The pencil markings from the back of the tracing paper will come off where you traced.

Step 6

6. Fold the paper as shown, so the fold goes through the animal's tail.

7. Turn over the paper and make another fold the same size as your first fold.

8. Continue folding your paper back and forth like an accordion until you reach the end.

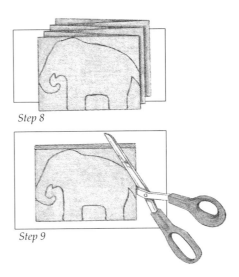
Step 8

Step 9

9. Hold the folded paper with the animal pattern facing up. Then cut along the lines of the animal pattern.

10. Unfold the paper, and you'll have a chain of paper animals! ☀

THE CIRCUS PARADE

When the Civil War began, 11 circuses and **menageries** *(me-NAJ-uh-rees), or collections of exotic animals, traveled around the country by horse-drawn wagon or by train. When the circus arrived in town, a parade created excitement and got people interested in going to see the show.*

PLAYTHINGS

A cloth doll made by a slave in Addy's time.

In Addy's time, children in slavery had few toys. They made their own toys or played with toys that older relatives had made for them. Girls like Addy made dolls from rags, corncobs, and even old wooden spoons. Because they had so few toys, slave children used their imaginations. Girls made "dollhouses" by drawing the rooms of a house in the dirt, and both boys and girls had fun riding sticks as if they were horses. Parents like Poppa sometimes made toys such as whistles and stilts out of wood scraps.

In cities, factories were just beginning to make children's toys. Machines made toys like cloth dolls, wooden building blocks, and china tea sets more quickly than they could be made by hand. And trains carried these toys to people all over America. Machine-made toys were less expensive than toys had been in the past, but families like Addy's still couldn't afford many of them.

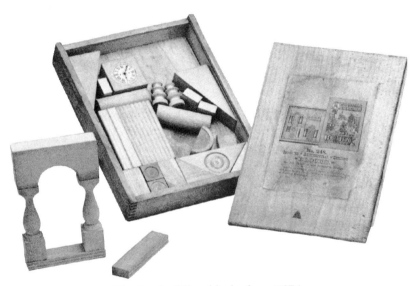

Wooden building blocks from 1874.

Poppa showed Addy and Sarah how to make shadow puppets so they could put on their own shadow play like the one they saw at church on Christmas. He even showed them how to make the puppets' arms move! Addy and Sarah decided to paint their puppets so they could play with them either behind a screen or without a screen. When the puppets were finished, Momma and Poppa tacked a sheet up in front of the sunny window in their room at the boarding house. Addy and Sarah slipped their puppets behind the sheet and put on a special shadow play just for them!

PLAYTHINGS

☀

Shadow Puppet

•

Jacob's Ladder

•

Hobbyhorse

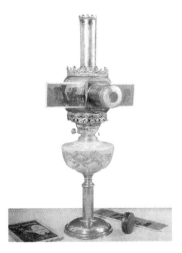

MAGIC LANTERNS
*When Addy was a girl, **magic lanterns** were popular toys. Magic lanterns were early slide projectors. Instead of using an electric light bulb, they used the light of a candle. Some magic lanterns could be attached to kerosene lamps like the one shown here. Children put a hand-painted glass slide into the viewer and the image was projected onto a wall.*

SHADOW PUPPET

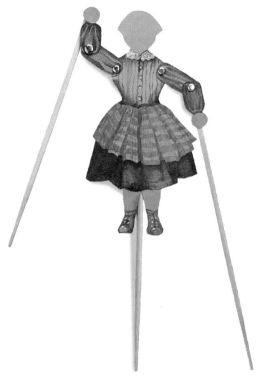

Tack a sheet in a sunny window, slip your puppet behind the sheet, and put on a shadow play just as Addy and Sarah did.

MATERIALS

Pencil
Sheet of tracing paper
Newspaper
Piece of poster board, 7 by 11 inches
Small knife
Scissors
4 brass fasteners*
Small artist's paintbrush
Acrylic paints, any colors
Wood glue
3 small sticks, each 10 inches long *(Thin bamboo or plastic chopsticks work well.)*

*Available in craft stores or in the school-supplies section of some department stores.

DIRECTIONS

1. Use the pencil to trace the puppet pattern pieces shown on the inside back cover of this book onto tracing paper. Don't cut them out.

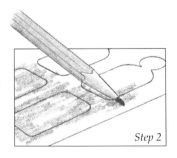

Step 2

2. Place the tracing paper onto newspaper, design side down. Use the side of the pencil to color over the lines of the pattern pieces.

3. Place the tracing paper on the poster board, design side up. Draw over the lines of the pattern pieces, pressing firmly.

4. Lift up the tracing paper. The pencil markings from the back of the tracing paper will come off where you traced.

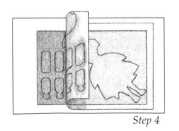

Step 4

5. Ask an adult to use the knife to cut out the small holes on the pattern pieces. Then cut out the pattern pieces.

6. To attach an arm, push a brass fastener through the hole in 1 of the lower arm pieces. Then push it through 1 of the holes in an upper arm piece. Fold the fastener flat.

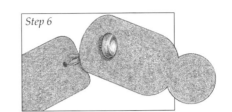

Step 6

7. Attach the arm to 1 of the puppet's shoulders with another brass fastener. Attach the other arm in the same way. Then paint your puppet.

8. After the paint has dried, lay your puppet on a table, with the back side facing up. Squeeze a line of glue down the middle of the puppet's back. Then squeeze a little glue on each of the puppet's hands.

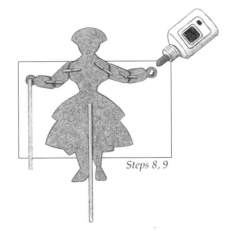

Steps 8, 9

9. Lay the sticks on the glue as shown. Let the glue dry completely.

10. To work your puppet, hold the middle stick in 1 hand. Use your other hand to move the puppet's arms. ☀

PAPER THEATERS

In Addy's time, some children made their own paper theaters by cutting out pictures of famous actors and playing with them on a paper stage. Paper theaters could also be bought in stores. Most theaters were in black and white, but people could also buy them in color.

JACOB'S LADDER

Tilt one block and watch the rest tumble!

MATERIALS

Fine sandpaper (150 grit)
4 blocks of wood, each 3 inches long,
  $2^1/2$ inches wide, and $1/2$ inch thick*
Foam paintbrush, 1 inch wide
Acrylic paint, any color
Hammer
12 flathead thumbtacks
3 pieces of $1/4$-inch-wide grosgrain ribbon,
  each 14 inches long
Scissors
Available in hardware and lumber stores.

DIRECTIONS

1. Sand the wood blocks until they are smooth. Dust off the blocks and then paint 1 side of each wood block with acrylic paint.

2. When the paint is dry, turn over the wood blocks and paint another side.

3. Keep painting until the blocks are painted on all sides. Add a second coat of paint if necessary.

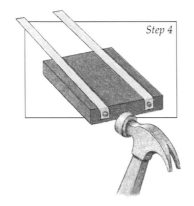
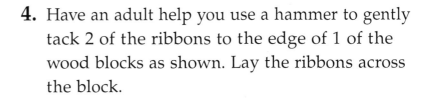

Step 4

4. Have an adult help you use a hammer to gently tack 2 of the ribbons to the edge of 1 of the wood blocks as shown. Lay the ribbons across the block.

5. Turn the wood block so the tacks are facing away from you.

6. Tack the other ribbon to the edge of the wood block, between the first 2 ribbons. Lay that ribbon across the block.

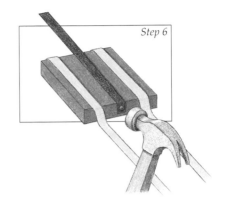

7. Place another wood block on top, with the ribbons in the middle. Let the ribbon tails hang out from the sides.

8. Fold 1 ribbon over the top block. Pull it tight and tack it to the edge of the top block. Pull up and tack the other 2 ribbons to the top block in the same way.

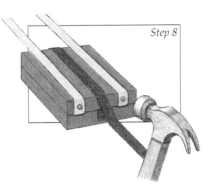

9. Repeat steps 7 and 8 for the last 2 wood blocks. Then trim off the extra ribbon. You will end up with a stack of 4 blocks connected by ribbons.

10. To play with your Jacob's Ladder, pick up the top block by its edges. Tilt the top block until it touches the second block. The block will look as if it's tumbling down. Watch closely to see how it works! ☀

The Fisk Jubilee Singers in the 1880s.

SPIRITUALS

Spirituals are religious songs that were first created by enslaved African Americans. "Climbing Jacob's Ladder" is a spiritual about a man named Jacob who dreamed he saw angels traveling up and down a ladder reaching to heaven. The Fisk Jubilee Singers, of Fisk University in Nashville, Tennessee, sang spirituals in the United States and Europe in Addy's time.

HOBBYHORSE

Gallop off on a hobbyhorse you make yourself!

MATERIALS

Foam paintbrush, 1 inch wide
Acrylic paints, any colors
3-foot wooden dowel, $5/8$ inch wide
Wooden head bead, $1\,7/16$ inches wide*
Pencil
Tracing paper
Scissors
2 pieces of felt, each 9 by 12 inches
Straight pins
Ruler
Thread
Needle
Wood glue
Polyester batting
Any of the following: buttons, tassels, yarn, cord
Head beads are wooden beads that have a hole drilled partially through them. They're usually used to make doll heads. They can be found in craft stores.

DIRECTIONS

1. Paint the dowel and the head bead. Set them aside to dry.

2. Use the pencil to trace the horse-head pattern on page 44 onto tracing paper. Then cut it out.

3. Put the 2 pieces of felt together and pin the pattern on the felt pieces. Cut around the pattern and then unpin it. Set the pattern aside.

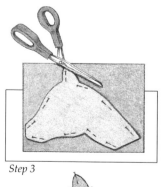

Step 3

4. Pin the edges of the 2 horse heads together.

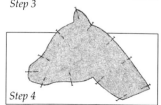

Step 4

5. Cut an 18-inch piece of thread, and then thread the needle. Tie a double knot near the other end of the thread.

6. Whipstitch your way up the back of the horse's neck. To whipstitch, come up at A. Then stitch over the edge to come up at B.

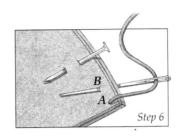
Step 6

7. Continue whipstitching until you've stitched around the horse's nose. Tie a knot close to your last stitch and cut off the extra thread. Then unpin the edges of the felt.

8. Squeeze a line of glue along the inside of the back of the horse's neck. Lay the dowel on top of the glue.

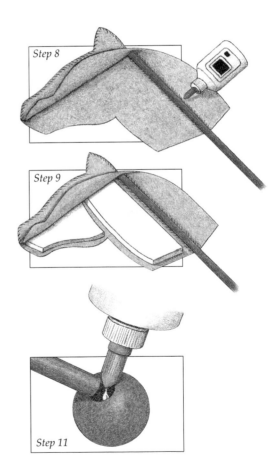
Step 8

Step 9

9. Tuck strips of batting inside the horse head. Pin the unfinished edges together.

10. Whipstitch from the horse's nose to the dowel. Tie a knot close to your last stitch and cut off the extra thread. Unpin the felt.

11. Glue the head bead onto the end of the dowel.

12. Now decorate your hobbyhorse! Glue on button eyes and tassels, or make cord reins and a yarn mane. ☀

Step 11

A STITCH IN TIME

Handmade clothes worn by slaves in Addy's time.

On Master Stevens's plantation, Addy's mother worked as a seamstress. She made clothes for Master Stevens's family, her own family, and for other slave families, too.

Enslaved women also made quilts. They sewed together scraps of material from old clothes and used raw cotton and bits of wool as filling. On one plantation, the sheep often ran through a brier patch. Slave women gathered the small tufts of wool stuck to the briers and used them as filling in their quilts.

Some women made quilts that used shapes and patterns they or their relatives remembered from Africa. A former slave named Harriet Powers made beautiful quilts that showed scenes from the Bible. Her quilt figures were very similar to the figures that people from the Fon, Ewe, Fanti, and Ashanti tribes sewed on their clothes and wall hangings in West Africa.

Harriet Powers made this Bible quilt in the 1880s.

When Addy and Momma escaped to freedom in Philadelphia, Momma went to work as a seamstress in Mrs. Ford's dress shop. Very few women in the 1860s could afford to have their clothes made at a dress shop. Most women made their families' clothes themselves, usually by taking apart old clothes and using the pieces as patterns.

While Momma and Mrs. Ford sewed dresses, Addy helped by making deliveries and sorting buttons. If Addy couldn't help with shop work, she took out her sewing bag. Inside she kept her needle book, thimble, and thread. She sewed, or *appliquéd*, small fabric shapes onto a square of plain blue cotton. Soon she would have a pretty appliquéd pillow for her bed!

A STITCH IN TIME

☀

Appliquéd Pillow

•

Drawstring Bag

•

Cross-Stitch Bookmark

SOJOURNER TRUTH

This 1864 picture shows Sojourner Truth with her knitting. In the 1790s, she was born into slavery in New York. In 1828, she became free when New York passed a law against slavery. Sojourner Truth was a courageous woman who traveled around the country to speak out against slavery.

APPLIQUÉD PILLOW

Use fabric appliqués to make your own personalized pillow!

MATERIALS

Pencil
3 sheets of white paper, each 8$\frac{1}{2}$ x 11 inches
Scissors
Fabric pen
Fabric scraps
2 pieces of solid-colored fabric, each 12 inches square
Straight pins
Thread
Ruler
Needle
Polyester stuffing

DIRECTIONS

1. Practice drawing simple patterns for your *appliqués*, or small fabric shapes, on the sheets of paper. Then cut out the paper patterns you want to use for your pillow.

Step 2

2. Use the fabric pen to trace your patterns onto the *wrong side*, or back side, of your fabric scraps. Cut out the shapes. You now have your appliqués!

Step 3

3. Lay 1 of the fabric squares on a table with the *right side*, or front side, facing up. Arrange the appliqués on the square and pin them down. Leave a $\frac{1}{2}$-inch border around the square.

4. Cut an 18-inch piece of thread, and then thread the needle. Tie a double knot near the other end of the thread.

5. Whipstitch the appliqués to the fabric square. To whipstitch, bring the needle up at A and stitch over the edge of the appliqué to go down at B. Come up at C and keep stitching!

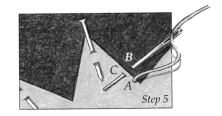

Step 5

6. When you finish, tie a knot on the underside of the fabric, close to your last stitch. Cut off the extra thread. Sew on the rest of your appliqués in the same way.

7. Remove the pins. Place the fabric square on the table with the appliquéd side facing up.

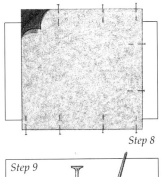

Step 8

8. Lay the other fabric square on top, with the wrong side facing up. Pin 3 edges together.

Step 9

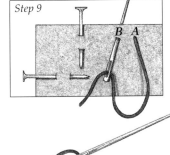

9. Sew a running stitch along these edges, $\frac{1}{4}$ inch from the edge. To sew running stitches, come up at A and go down at B.

10. Then come up at C and go down at D. Make smaller running stitches at the corners. When you've finished all 3 sides, tie a knot close to your last stitch and cut off the extra thread.

Step 10

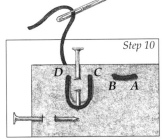

11. Unpin the fabric. Turn the pillow right side out and fill it with stuffing.

12. Fold in both sides of the last edge and pin them together. Whipstitch this side closed. Then unpin the edges, and your pillow is finished! ☀

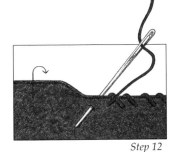

Step 12

DRAWSTRING BAG

Addy kept her sewing supplies in a pretty drawstring bag.

MATERIALS

Pencil
Tracing paper
Scissors
Piece of fabric, 18 by 12 inches
Straight pins
Fabric pen
Ruler
Thread
Needle
Tassel
Piece of ¼-inch cord or ribbon, 24 inches long
Safety pin
2 macramé beads, each ½ inch wide

DIRECTIONS

1. Use the pencil to trace the pattern shown on page 43 onto tracing paper. Trace the Xs, too. Cut out the pattern.

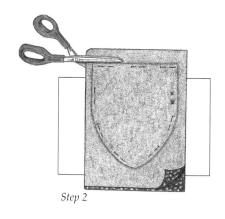

Step 2

2. Fold the fabric in half, with the *right side*, or front side, facing in. Pin the pattern to the fabric, and then cut around it. Unpin the pattern. You now have 2 pieces of fabric!

3. On the wrong side of 1 piece, use the fabric pen to make 2 Xs, as shown on the pattern. Pin the 2 fabric pieces together with the right sides facing each other.

4. Cut an 18-inch piece of thread, and then thread the needle. Tie a double knot near the other end of the thread.

5. Sew the 2 curved sides of the bag together with a running stitch $1/2$ inch from the edge. Have the fabric piece with the Xs facing up. To sew running stitches, come up at A and go down at B. Then come up at C and go down at D.

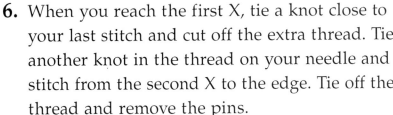

Step 5

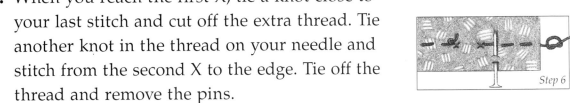

Step 5

6. When you reach the first X, tie a knot close to your last stitch and cut off the extra thread. Tie another knot in the thread on your needle and stitch from the second X to the edge. Tie off the thread and remove the pins.

Step 6

7. Fold down the top edge of the bag 2 inches. Pin it as shown.

Step 7

8. Hold the bag open with 1 hand, and sew a running stitch $1/2$ inch from the folded edge at the top of the bag. Tie a knot close to your last stitch. Sew another row of running stitches $1/2$ inch below the first row.

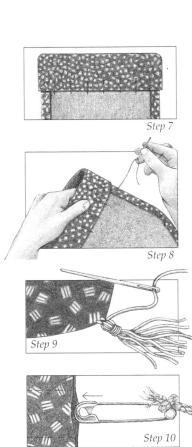

Step 8

9. Turn your bag right side out. Sew a tassel on the bottom of the bag.

Step 9

10. Tie 1 end of the cord or ribbon to the end of a closed safety pin. Insert the pin into the slit. Slide the pin all the way around until you can pull it out the other side of the slit.

Step 10

11. Cut the cord from the safety pin. Tie a knot 3 inches from each end of the cord. Slip 1 bead onto each end of the cord, and then tie another knot after each bead. Pull the beads to close the bag so your treasures won't fall out! ☀

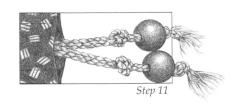

Step 11

CROSS-STITCH BOOKMARK

Addy used leftover ribbon from Mrs. Ford's shop to make a bookmark for her friend Sarah.

MATERIALS

Piece of 11-count cross-stitch canvas, 3 by 8 inches
Ruler
Fabric pen with disappearing ink
Scissors
Embroidery floss, 2 different colors
Needle
White thread
10 inches of grosgrain ribbon, $2^1/4$ inches wide

DIRECTIONS

1. Lay the canvas on a table. At the upper left corner, measure 1 inch in from the side and 1 inch down from the top.

Step 2

2. With the fabric pen, make a small "X" on the square where your measured lines come together. This will be the top left corner of the capital "F."

3. Follow the pattern on page 42 to mark the rest of the design on the canvas with your fabric pen. Each square on the pattern equals 1 square on the canvas. Count carefully!

Step 4

4. Cut an 18-inch piece of floss. The floss is made up of 6 strands. To cross-stitch, separate 2 strands.

5. Thread the needle with those 2 strands. Tie a double knot near the other end of the floss.

6. Begin by stitching the border around the bookmark. To cross-stitch, come up at A and go down at B.

7. Then come up at C and go down at D. You just made your first "cross"!

8. When you make several stitches in a row, you can make half of all the stitches first, and then go back and "cross" them.

9. When you finish cross-stitching the border, turn to the back of the canvas and slip the needle under 4 stitches. Cut off the extra floss.

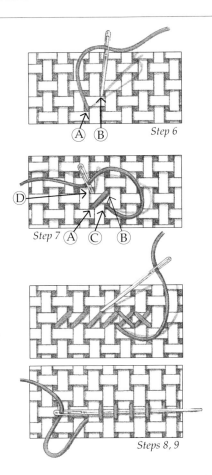

Step 6

Step 7 Ⓐ Ⓒ Ⓑ

Steps 8, 9

10. Use the other color of floss to cross-stitch the letters, starting with the capital "F."

11. When you finish stitching, cut around your cross-stitched design just outside the border.

12. With white thread, sew the cross-stitched canvas onto the ribbon with a running stitch. To sew a running stitch, come up at A and then go down at B.

13. Then come up at C and go down at D. When you've finished, tie a knot on the underside of the bookmark, close to your last stitch.

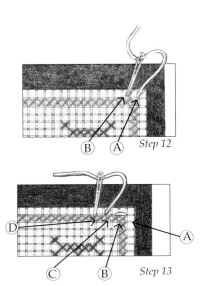

Step 12

Step 13

14. Finish the bookmark by trimming a "V" into each end of the ribbon. ☀

GAMES

Enslaved field workers harvesting sugar cane.

When Addy was enslaved on Master Stevens's plantation, she didn't have much time to play games. She worked hard helping Auntie Lula in the kitchen. In the middle of each morning and afternoon she also carried water buckets to the field workers so they could have a drink. Whenever she brought water, she hoped to see her brother Sam. He was always ready with a riddle or a joke to make her laugh.

Children in slavery who were old enough to work were allowed to play only at night after the workday was over or on Sundays, when there was no work. Most of their play didn't require any equipment. Children sometimes drew a large ring in the dirt. Then they danced inside the ring, clapping their hands while they sang their favorite rhymes. Some enslaved children made their own balls out of rags wrapped with thread, and they made their own marbles out of clay.

In Philadelphia, Addy had little room to play. Buildings were crowded together, and the streets were filled with wagons and streetcars. Addy and Sarah played games like hopscotch and jump rope on the sidewalk, and they played tag in city parks or in the school yard, just as you do today.

Some of Addy's school lessons were like games, too. For math, Miss Dunn sometimes had students work with her tangram puzzle. It had seven pieces called *tans*. Students used the tans to make fancy shapes like *pentagons*, which have five sides. Addy and Sarah loved working with the tangram puzzle. When they finished making the assigned shapes, Miss Dunn let them create shapes of their own!

GAMES

❋

Changeable Pictures

•

Tangram

•

Jump Rope

GAMES THAT TEACH

*In Addy's time, it was illegal for people in slavery in the South to go to school. But some black children learned their numbers by playing games like **Old Hundred**, or hide-and-seek, with white children. To play, one child covers her eyes and counts to one hundred while the other children hide.*

Books with pictures made learning to read easier and more fun.

CHANGEABLE PICTURES

Addy played with changeable pictures to create dozens of funny-looking people!

MATERIALS

Scissors
6 full-length magazine pictures of people, all about the
   same size and no larger than 3 by 5 inches each
6 unlined index cards, each 3 by 5 inches
White glue
Ruler
Pencil
Small bowl
Foam paintbrush

DIRECTIONS

1. Carefully cut out the magazine pictures of people.

2. Lay an index card on the table. Glue 1 of the pictures onto the index card. Smooth over the picture with your fingers so you won't have any air bubbles.

3. Use the ruler and pencil to draw a line across the index card that divides the legs of the magazine picture from the body.

4. Now use the ruler and pencil to draw a line across the index card that divides the head from the body.

5. Cut along the pencil lines. You will end up with 3 cards—1 with the head, 1 with the body, and 1 with the legs.

Steps 3, 4, 5

6. Glue the other 5 magazine pictures to the rest of the index cards and follow steps 3 through 5 to cut them apart in the same way.

Step 7

7. Squeeze a little glue into the bowl. Dip the paintbrush into the glue, and then brush a thin layer of glue over the front of each card. The glue will look milky at first, but it will dry clear.

8. Let the glue dry for about 15 minutes. Then add another coat of glue.

9. When the last coat of glue is dry, you're ready to play with your changeable pictures. Mix and match the cards to make as many funny combinations as you can! ☀

CHANGEABLE LANDSCAPE

Another changing picture game from Addy's time is called Endless Changes of Landscape, or Myriorama (meer-ee-uh-RA-ma). Children could rearrange the nine hand-painted panels to create hundreds of different landscapes.

TANGRAM

*See how many different shapes you can make with the **tans**, or pieces of this puzzle!*

MATERIALS

Pencil
Ruler
Piece of poster board, 6 inches square
Black ballpoint pen
Scissors
Small artist's paintbrush
Acrylic paint, any color

DIRECTIONS

1. Use the pencil and ruler to mark 3 dots along the bottom of 1 side of the poster board, 1½ inches apart.

2. Mark the other 3 sides of the square in the same way.

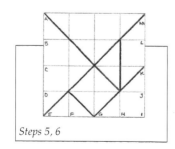

Step 3

3. Line up your ruler along 2 dots that are across from each other. Lightly draw a pencil line to connect the 2 dots.

4. Connect the rest of the dots in the same way. You will end up with a grid of 16 squares.

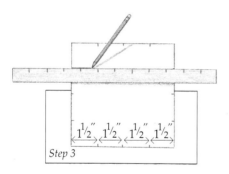

Steps 5, 6

5. Use the pencil to lightly letter the corners of the squares as shown, using letters A through M.

6. Use the ruler and black pen to draw the darker lines shown on the pattern at left.

7. Cut the poster board along the black lines. You'll have 7 shapes, or *tans*.

8. Paint 1 side of the tans and then let them dry for about 15 minutes.

9. Give the tans another coat of paint so you no longer see your pen and pencil lines.

10. Now you're ready to play Tangram. You must use all 7 tans to make a design, and none of the tans can overlap. Try a few of your own designs.

11. Once you've got the hang of it, see if you can make some of the designs shown on the cards below. Then try to put the tans back together in a square! ☀

THREE WAYS TO PLAY

Tangram is a Chinese puzzle game brought to the United States in the early 1800s. People used the tans in three ways. Some people in Addy's time used them to solve math problems. But most people had fun trying to copy shapes like those shown on the tangram cards at left, or just using their imaginations to create their own designs!

JUMP ROPE

Make a simple jump rope to play with by yourself or with friends!

MATERIALS

Piece of rope, at least 7 feet long
Scissors
Ruler
2 macramé beads, each 1$\frac{1}{2}$ inches wide

DIRECTIONS

1. Find the right length for your jump rope by standing in the middle of the rope and raising it in your hands until your hands are even with your shoulders. Cut off the excess length.

2. Tie a knot about 5 inches from 1 end of the rope.

3. Slide a macramé bead onto that end of the rope until it rests on the knot. Then tie another knot to hold the bead in place. Cut off the extra tail of rope.

4. Tie a knot in the other end of the rope so that the length is comfortable for you when you jump. Then tie the other macramé bead onto this end of the rope in the same way.

5. If you're jumping rope by yourself, try hopping on 1 foot and then the other. Or try jumping rope backward!

6. If you're jumping rope with friends, try 1 of the jump rope games on the next page.

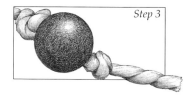

Step 1

Step 3

CAT'S CRADLES

*Children in Addy's time made **cat's cradles**, or string figures. Children sometimes wove string figures to go along with stories they were telling.*

ROCK THE BOAT (3 OR MORE PLAYERS)

1. Pick 2 players to be the first rope turners. Have them each hold 1 end of the rope.

2. The rope turners swing the rope back and forth, not overhead. The shape the rope makes as it swings back and forth looks like the bottom of a boat.

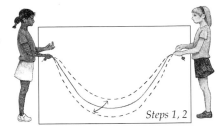

Steps 1, 2

3. Each player must enter the "boat," jump the rope twice, and then jump out without catching her feet in the rope.

Step 3

4. If a player does catch her feet in the rope, she becomes a rope turner.

AROUND THE CLOCK (UP TO 13 PLAYERS)

1. A player holds the rope by 1 end. The rest of the rope stretches out before her, like a hand of a clock.

Steps 1, 2, 3

2. The rest of the players form a circle around her, like the numbers on a clock.

3. The player in the middle turns around, swinging the rope in a circle, low to the ground. The other players jump the rope when it comes their way.

4. If a player misses a jump, she takes the place of the player in the middle. To make the game more challenging, raise the rope higher! ☀

PATTERNS

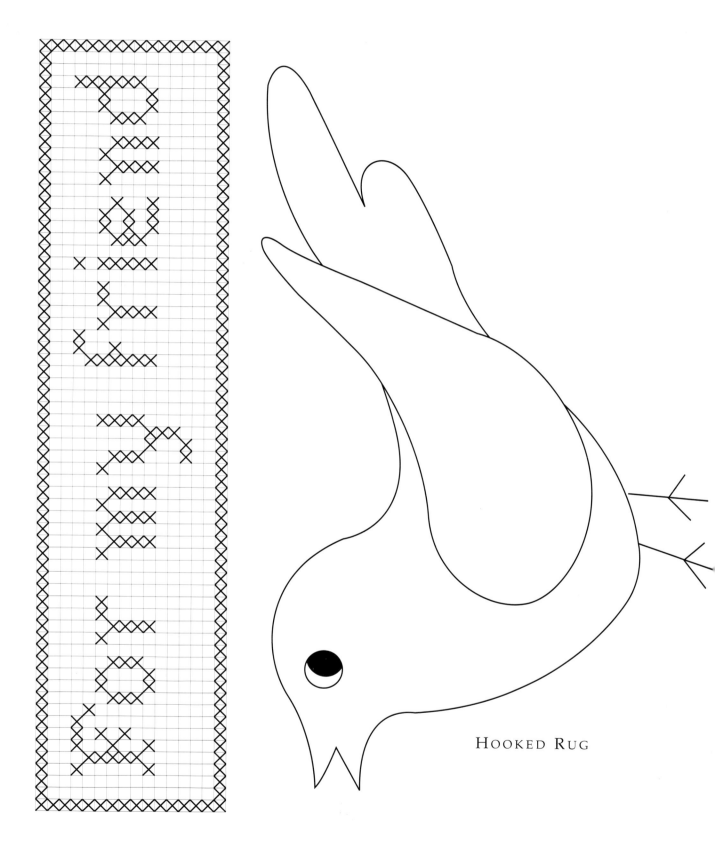

BOOKMARK

HOOKED RUG

DRAWSTRING BAG

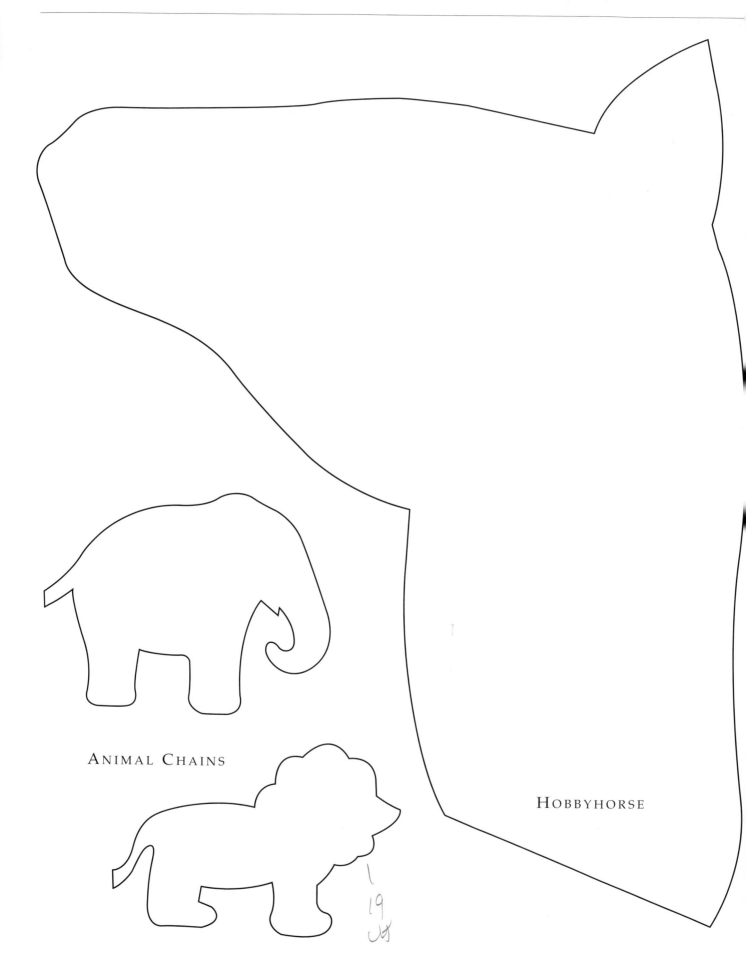

Animal Chains

Hobbyhorse